False Memory

TONY LOPEZ is the author of 20 books of poetry, fiction and criticism. His most recent poetry collections are *Devolution* (The Figures, USA) and *Data Shadow* (Reality Street, UK), both published in 2000. His work is featured in many anthologies including *Twentieth-Century British & Irish Poetry* (Oxford), *Other* (Wesleyan) and *Conductors of Chaos* (Picador). He is well-known as a poetry performer and has given readings throughout UK, Europe and North America. He teaches in England at the University of Plymouth, where he was appointed the first professor of poetry in 2000.

Also by Tony Lopez

Poetry
    Devolution (The Figures, 2000)
    Data Shadow (Reality Street, 2000)
    False Memory (The Figures, 1996)
    Negative Equity (Equipage, 1995)
    Stress Management (Boldface Press, 1994)
    A Theory of Suplus Labour (Curiously Strong, 1990)
    A Handbook of British Birds (Pig Press, 1982)
    Abstract & Delicious (Secret Books, 1982)
    Change (New London Pride, 1978)
    The English Disease (Skyline Press, 1978)
    Snapshots (Oasis Books, 1976)

Criticism
    The Poetry of W. S. Graham (Edinburgh University Press, 1989)

False Memory

Tony Lopez

SALT

PUBLISHED BY SALT PUBLISHING
PO Box 937, Great Wilbraham, Cambridge PDO CB1 5JX United Kingdom
PO Box 202, Applecross, Western Australia 6153

All rights reserved

© Tony Lopez, 2003

The right of Tony Lopez to be identified as the
author of this work has been asserted by him in accordance
with Section 77 of the Copyright, Designs and Patents Act 1988.

This book is in copyright. Subject to statutory exception
and to provisions of relevant collective licensing agreements,
no reproduction of any part may take place without the written
permission of Salt Publishing.

First published 2003

Printed and bound in the United Kingdom by Lightning Source

Typeset in Swift 9.5 / 13

This book is sold subject to the conditions that it shall not,
by way of trade or otherwise, be lent, re-sold, hired out,
or otherwise circulated without the publisher's prior consent
in any form of binding or cover other than that in which
it is published and without a similar condition including this
condition being imposed on the subsequent purchaser.

ISBN 1 84471 030 0 paperback

SP

1 3 5 7 9 8 6 4 2

for Sara

Contents

Corneal Erosion	1
Studies in Classic American Literature	11
Assembly Point D	21
Blue Shift	31
Non-Core Assets	41
Brought Forward	51
Imitation of Life	61
Restricted Zone (slight return)	71
Speckled Noise	81
Always Read the Label	91
Radial Symmetry	101
Index	113

Acknowledgments

Acknowledgements and thanks to the Harold Hyam Wingate Foundation for a Wingate Scholarship which enabled the composition of this work; to Geoffrey Young for the publication of the chapbook *False Memory* (The Figures, 1996); to Ken Edwards for *Data Shadow* (Reality Street, 2000); also to the late great Richard Caddel, to Hélène Aji, Macgregor Card, Kelvin Corcoran, Henri Deluy, Nate Dorward, Andrew Duncan, Edward Foster, John Kinsella, Ross Leckie, Peter Manson, Andrew Maxwell, Anthony Mellors, Peter Middleton, Robin Purves, Peter Quartermain, Ian Robinson, Iain Sinclair, Simon Smith, John Tranter and Keith Tuma who have published poems from this book in *Action Poétique, Angel Exhaust, Capilano Review, The Fiddlehead, Fragmente, The Germ: A Journal of Poetic Research, The Gig, Jacket, Oasis, Object Permanence, Salt* and *Talisman*, in pamphlets from Equipage and Short Run Press and in the anthologies *Conductors of Chaos* (Picador, 1996), *Other* (Wesleyan, 1999) and *Twentieth-Century British & Irish Poetry* (Oxford, 2001).

Cover drawing, "Interface," 2002, by Steve di Benedetto, courtesy of Derek Eller Gallery and A. G. Rosen.

Corneal Erosion

And I don't see how we can win. The first faint
Intermittent soundings of the sirens may be ignored
Just as the slogans come through unpractised speech.
In Arcadia, when I was there, I did not see hammering stone
But you should vacate the building when you hear
A continuous note. It is best to move away –
Best to pay bills by direct debit and avoid offices.
Water bombs, I hear, are great fun and completely harmless.
We have the numbers 12, 84 and 51 mostly
Counters, cashiers and other people. Stay at home
Stay in bed, shop through TV: I should say so.
Think about who is at the wheel in the car ahead.
At the time I was interrupted by a lady from Totnes
Who had been burgled and who couldn't keep quiet.

I would like a no-risk enrolment (ring your choice).
A day on which a raven flew high overhead
Brought in the vogue for apparently fenceless gardens.
I heard the call, looked up, went on with my work
Turning an adjustable. It was the enclosures acts
Where maize is planted right up to the treatment works.
Magazine fillers, non-fiction, writing for children,
Do you have the time for the due process of law?
The air itself is carved into sectors maintained
By threat of force and the stony faced use of finance
In a pre-paid tunnel of exclusion going away.
The animals get eaten or plucked from the sky.
Don't be fooled by pretty flowered frocks and bifocals
Some of these old people are dangerous criminals.

Little goats soon exhausted the blue-flowered alfalfa
And bitter willow. We had chestnuts and new cheese on offer,
October it was. A wave running through the house. I woke
Going back to the engine over the Somerset levels.
Best if we call it a 'maintenance holiday'
And patch in warm associations. Arrange for prosody
To look over the tapes. Allude to pleasant hopes and dreams.
This could be the last decision of the outgoing
Management. Give me the LD50 on leakage projections –
But make it verbal, beware the shredder, better burn this.
A tree here and there on the fire horizon.
Planes light up for an instant and then flash again,
Further on. Most of the eastern counties are now flooded
But the troubles keep us moving in sparse woodland

Or what used to be called campus development
Before the fires. Fields of cars reflect heat. Hazard fence
And all-over schleiren: a metal surfaced plant
Or planet. We ride in lively annelid segments
Under London, past corrugated sheds of steel
And loaded trucks of used aggregate, ready to move out
For in-fill in the home counties. How does it feel
To be really on the make at last? Local sea trout
Close to extinction, look likely for bio-production
If we can get the lice off their backs. It is lightning
Regenerates the forests. Zeus solves the equation
By being a name that encodes what is frightening.
It's good to be at work, to inhabit some other place,
But would you pay for a job title and office space?

Me neither. Though it depends what you mean by *pay*.
Cash is the least of it, since one's life is used up in attendance.
You may find it more convenient to insert Greek characters
Than built-in negated symbols. Use keyboard shortcuts
But avoid slash and burn diacritical embellishments.
These templates are used for creating radicals:
Ask Annie Apple, Oscar Orange, Yo-yo Man. In French,
As any major dude will tell you, gender is proclaimed
By a particular use of adjectives and past participles.
Each time you say you don't believe in the unified subject
Another child enters the symbolic order. Clap hands,
Do not adjust your seats, extinguish smoking materials:
We're going down to Shanty town. Expect some slippage.
Bourgeois is an obsolete type size, pronounced *berjoyce*.

Of course the search committee and shortlist were bourgeois,
The process itself has built in defences against slippage.
Now the way is clear for open cast extraction of materials
The growth would be more visible if it were on your hands.
We did not know enough to resent being called subjects
So dazzled were we by synecdoche. Each party seeks Paul:
A name that I didn't even have to make up. *Proclaimed
Land* is a book title for Lacanians who work in French
That I offer here for free and without strings. Radicals
Are subject to growth deformation by embellishment.
You never see the road itself if you're on a shortcut.
I have every sympathy for those who wipe out characters
But deferred closure is our only chance of attendance
When we finally step out of the taxi and begin to play.

Rally cries are paralysed before your eyes.
It's the knowledge that truth is simple, natural and final
That brings them to their feet. Electric Elgar:
Lillies that fester at party conference.
Good mottled and stripy waves curling on sand
That's how I see it. Sailing in the gravel pit
Doing the rest of it right here in my mind.
Mobile homes close to the site entrance, on set aside,
Landscaped in. Nicely printed day permits, some fat carp.
A part-work on angling (with free binder) in the Sierra,
8% gilts. What a way to invest our redundancy.
Services may be altered to accommodate changes in demand.
A bright young man, well schooled, from a good home
Takes the platform to sustained applause from all sides.

The pills are trapped between clear orange plastic and foil
In sheets of twelve, long and rounded, easy to swallow.
We are still waiting for the peace dividend
But would settle for fixed-rate income in the interim.
In court, out of court, AGM, shareholders meeting –
Exactly what does it cost to set up a shelter belt
Or property trust? For dinner we have turkey franks
Unless you want me to stir fry. Major's majority.
So you have a stoma and here you are telling me
It's best to keep your pants on when you have sex
In case you spill the shit. Check on the pantograph
Running seven minutes late out of Berwick-upon-Tweed,
Structure is fully visible only late in construction
And weatherproofing will obscure its own means of support.

Drunk in a sauna out in the snowy woods
I saw a meteor shower or satellite wreckage
Then ribbons of metal foil falling into the sea.
I mean how can you measure functional accuracy
Unless you have a position? A sudden flight of geese
Progressing at five knots across the channel. What you see
Is not the outline but the size and speed of the signal,
It is a matter of blocking impulse transport.
Light picks up reflective matter on the screen:
That which adheres only to damaged tissues.
Since 28 appears twice on yellow brick, I see
That it cannot be a sundial or a plan of rooms.
Radio tracking through the shadowy forest
Even the experts rarely see pine martens.

Watch out for PROSPECT on a pillar to the right
Of the entrance. A blue beam picks out yellow dye.
Attending to what is actually there in the suburbs
Slow green and red flares move across the sky.
A small force of planes pretends to be an invasion fleet
Carrying Indian names into the air. I'll meet you
In the Eagle and puzzle at numbers fixed to the wall
Where wolves howl and reindeers run. The fit is on.
We mention one absent far to the north, imagine,
The premises are protected by a Minerva alarm system
And sky tints vary according to the position of panes.
Since 28 appears twice on yellow brick, say it:
You are as old as you feel - but how well does your DNA copy?
You can't substitute for okra in a ground-nut stew.

Studies in Classic American Literature

Walking on the crusty surface, coming back
I heard a voice from way inside saying
"Start as you mean to go on" with calm authority.
Slack as any boy on hourly pay, let's wait and see,
To see what the pill boxes are for just here:
So many wires strung out over the land.
Whereas what I find immediately striking
Is the vibration of ill-fitting window trim,
The muted zip of foliage and cloud.
But the take-off gives the plane away and turns
All four propellers over gun slits in grey
Now frost-etched and crumbly, blind and dumb,
In fields that under high ridges are resplendent
In apple green / Autumn tints / snowy white.

Signs poke up among large dripping Friesian patches:
Wholesale electrical distributors, freehold for sale.
I pray with speed put on your woodland dress
We leave the boundaries and sweet gardens of home,
Virgil knew all about ethnic cleansing.
The ability to work with change is at a premium
A bottle of frizz-ease, the five-minute manager –
That phrase was meat from the butcher's slab.
Stand by, put your hands over your eyes, revise,
Think carefully about your statement. Could this be
A cereal ad, digitally remastered? Think big.
The product message, phrased in affirmatives,
Sprouts from wicket fences in quality time.
If you'd like to know more, please turn up your volume now.

Irish box, leather boats, seafaring monks
The heavy swell lifts the ship and slams it down,
Molluscs that change sex because of boat paint.
Rum and black, mud in your eye, tarry old Jack
Star-gazy pie, stab you in the back, old crow
Old soak, old salty dog – breaking the surface
But keeping low, water halfway up the mask.
It's cold, dark, you see lights along the water's edge.
The ship leaves its wake on water and steams on :
It is impossible to explain the meaning of art.
Mist gathers, as if we're already far out to sea
Long after the quotas have gone, fish all fished out.
That is when a man is capable of being in uncertainties
Eliminating large areas of the original image.

I saw cables going down into the Atlantic
From a small sandy cove like a memory.
Lookouts at the windows with binoculars,
Maybe a radar scanner moving round on the roof.
The feel of this is early modern, menacing
And laden with myth: Rex Warner in old leather.
That the treasure of a nation is its equity.
Grainy blow-ups of lightning bolts on white walls,
Almost everyone in England writes poetry, imagine.
Wind rattling the windows, spray streams on glass,
Is there a way to test this recovered memory?
What is the point of all this stuff about fish?
Maurice Saatchi's hat, bonfire of the quangos.
The rosy bracts of bougainvillaea.

It's a psilocybin-cocaine mix called *Atlantic High*,
We have no current memory of those events.
Her binoculars were found to be full of sand,
A stash of electric-shock batons on the roof –
A menacing pause as they re-arm and re-group.
The back room is full of specialist rubber and leather,
We should remember Mrs Thatcher for "equity release."
Imagine all the people having enough to eat.
The special relationship made us truly great,
City blocks of broken glass, system collapse,
I had a lead on the False Memory Society.
Fish fingers pushed into knitted gloves
Better make pickles with unripe quangos
Bougainvillaea sounds like a great place to live.

They came like shadows through the Alleghenies
Reading *Pittsburgh Memoranda* (Sante Fe, 1935)
Bombed streets made a great playground for the kids.
I hear the Princess of Wales is reading *Moby Dick*.
The product wants development at this stage,
Needs characters: Berrigan, Peel-Off, Hell's Own Vendor –
How about the Robinson Jeffers Summer Surfing School?
It would have to be individual tuition I guess.
They say leading black Democrats want to release
Golf courses for building homes. Are there black golfers?
"Some circumstantial evidence is very strong,"
Thoreau said, "as when you find a trout in the milk."
Ronald and Nancy with their dog in leash-tow,
Moving, smiling and waving at the TV camera.

By pressing a piece of paper on top of the inky block
From Cape Cod to the Gulf, the fisheries gone.
He came to this estate to interview or witness
And has too many B2s already, no offence.
One of those shirts with a contrasting collar,
Old sweaty ash smell. A new business plan
With wooden sleds, rolled felt, ex-army torches
Clearing a war-zone in weeks. Rubble disposal.
The visit made a great and lasting impression
His style being formal, mechanical and flat,
For a whale ship was his Yale college and his Harvard.
He arrived and left in an ambulance, was locked
Into a loft with a coyote, newspapers, a walking stick.
It was always there, only now you look up, the sea.

If the skin is tougher than anticipated
We must apply more pressure; if it is thicker,
We maintain the pressure for a longer time.
Orange peel perhaps, or scars from leg irons:
I'm looking at performance indicators for performance art.
Writing on a continuous strip of paper which unrolls
Forging Pound's pre-Raphaelite *Cantos*, inventing
Chinese characters, neat planks, Helvetica type.
Just how did polenta become an alpine food?
They were pulled out of their cars and shot by the road
In front of the cameras, a half moon in the afternoon sky.
It was always there, only now you look up, the source.
He was completely white, as if just dusted, bone and skin
Looking at the wasp going into the ground, down there,
Carrying the seed of a Eucalyptus to St Elizabeth's.

A small female passenger in a dark blue tracksuit
With embroidered fruits and flowers and Latin names,
White socks and moccasin style casual shoes
Nos patriam fugimus: a man in a cage
Being flown back from Italy to America.
One of those imprinted mammals in the nocturnal house:
Tired routines, a birth video onstage, performers
Intending, I believe, to drive out the audience
Who were too dull or too polite to move from their seats
At say £100 return. Snatches of Wagner
Lying in a bookshelf in anorexic trance –
Travelling once again in a time of great floods.
"Are you writing your memoirs?" the officer said.
Prunus avium, if I remember, criminally insane

And in sole charge of the American epic.
Early horizontal morning light strikes a deer
Looking back from a field at the train going by.
Black fingers push through housing project wire
In the city jail, some kind of hard-boiled scenario,
Without any irritable reaching after fact and reason.
Shells crash into the Presidential palace which burns
Orange and black. Another truckload of volunteers
Is going to reinforce the frontline against tanks.
Three prisoners recaptured on the Isle of Wight.
The production of beauty was never a more
Urgent necessity. Snow on marble (*Apuane*),
Some indication of the heights beyond:
Your name will not be revealed without your permission.

Assembly Point D

Dauntless the slug-horn to my lips I set
Taking a stand for the names who had been
So badly treated by crowd behaviour in the market;
Whereas our man was calm, drew figures in the sand,
And spoke to them as individuals. The old guy
Putters on, his canvas in a trench, putting neat squiggles
On the big white primed sheets: a million each, believe it.
Cartoon prawns and crabs go into Eurotunnel
Singing along with zydeco music. Redwoods fall.
It was a teacher bound and gagged a four-year-old boy
With sticky tape labelled *Nastro Adesivo: 3M*
Holding back the late works to keep up the selling price.
Can you design a machine that turns coffee
Into urine? That daydreams of oral sex?

Our fortunes are in the stars, truly, since brokers
Are using astrology in the stockmarket. What price
Celestial backwardation (a little space to write and eat salad in)?
Shadowing the wives of ex-company presidents
In their dotage. The owl of Minerva begins her flight
Only as dusk is falling. My nerves are bad tonight.
This kind of gives closure to a long career in "Vice."
All famous names, all massive savings, every third one free.
The office has a fine view of cliffs and grassy hills.
You read INDUS OPAQUE as you stick out your tongue
Over where a new vine is beginning to cover the gazebo
Cut so many times before. [Clay animal noses here.]
Rose garden : black velvet : stalking donkey :
The banquet is at 3102 Main Street, 15th and Main.

A thread goes through the book, I don't mean ideas, but each
Gathering of four sheets sewn into sixteen pages
Which are I suppose ideas, even those that are blanks.
Autumn walks in the poem as a goddess, an idea
But also (because she is a goddess) good to eat and rollover with.
I was not so impressed with the chicken dinner after all,
You eat with your fingers and get sticky round the mouth.
It is not Autumn at all, she comes home with groceries
And gets into a hot bath. I think in Bonnard reproductions,
Mosaics with drips of water running on the little stones.
Spaghetti vongole appeals to me more than clam chowder.
I was born in the city but I don't live there now,
Can't afford it. This *is* the subtext of *After Lorca*:
Swimming pools, mirrors, the denial of the father.

Three black bears on a green T-shirt from Canada
It might be that a new colony was begun, distorted
If I remember by flaking plaster - so that what you see
Is a non-representational blackbird that was happening
At breakfast. It seems to be the time for questions. Not yet.
Geometrical flowers on a soft-shaded plastic tablecloth
With a grey design something like strawberry leaves.
One night the termites fly and are sexually active
I mean not fancy envelopes but business envelopes
Such as the enclosed renewal-notice. Countless aphids.
I put them down one after another and the effect
Was moulded in the glass. So we are the New Abjectionists
And maybe one or two pairs are successful up there
Have you seen the patterns on the insides of envelopes?

We were shredding gangster biographies in the backroom
Working most nights. My job was to put in the obvious
Rip-off that blinded those marks to the bare-faced
Totality of the scam. We'd admit a little steal or two
And call it "literary allusion" – now is that high class or what?
Steve Benson and Jean Day were playing on the tape recorder.
Diagonal rows of circles with quarters of dark blue
And then circles with white slots like NO ENTRY signs,
Then both of these patterns reversed. That is where
We must remove the tiles hoping the walls stay up –
All those wings in the sky, it was so pretty to see.
But since that branch fell on me I must always be working:
We use chemical sex-signals to protect apples
And have forgotten how to relax. Down at the mouth

As if somehow in the fifties it just popped out
Like one of those cartoon light-bulb ideas. Oh sure.
And in those days it was paste-up or shut up
If you catch my drift: translation rights, short-term options.
These dupes think that Burroughs invented the cut-up
By spreading his payments over four months. *New dawn,
Danse du feu, Handel, Albertine, Rosa Mundi.*
Since then I have begun to set up a new project
It is only there for the reverse print that you barely see:
The ideal appears and reconstructs the real world
Into the shape of an intellectual realm. Even so
He proves he is a brave leader by resigning.
My favourite is an unknown yellow with blackspot
Have you completed all of the sections?

I believe this blue is the newest colour and good enough
For the conference backdrop. I wanted to include
A wheelbarrow just for the hell of it. Hello Horace.
Having waited in all day for the gas men
I was working up a panic attack alone in the house.
All very neo-rural: introspective subjectivity,
Whereas what we have here is a cheap ventriloquist routine
Which ought to hold down the "Care in the Community"
    budget.
Really high tech, no doors, you just bale out the back:
Soon we may re-label "breakdown" as an ordinary life-event
Which is the proper response to current social conditions.
Of the blackbird, only two feet remained on the hedge.
Beside me this famished shadow does gnaw the joy away –
Would you go down on his donut? This ain't rock and roll,

Erasures and palimpsests are reduced to a flat
Surface effect: the afterlife of ethics.
A judge, a game-show host, bag-lady, dinner-lady,
Madman, murderer, banished king, politician,
Football manager, dentist, spoilt birthday-girl.
A few poor tatterdemalions made all this racket,
Howling in the night. Ugolino was there
Chewing a juicy walnut of brains from behind,
His arse positioned over the stunned polis.
Sing poor, sweet airlines. Scholars have paid lip-service
To the oral nature of poetry. We can see
Submissive women waiting on TV mountain tops:
Lovely silk dress in a helicopter shot. You'll need
Your velour passenger pillow and something to read.

Every so often the day builds around a menu
Say taking stock from the freezer for a *risotto*
Or calling early at the fish stall: oysters on ice.
Let's eat again real soon. I would be happy to go
With that old authentic abstract expressionist work
If we could print it on plastic. We're looking at
A futures market in concept art. You could hedge
Against primitives or streetnics or property as such,
Get in at zero and the only way is up.
White image of a plane on a blue ground
Then pull back to route on map of North America.
Eventually the loss of loss, fear of experience
(Tanks in European forests) writing *The Georgics*
When civil war had destroyed the culture itself.

This turning seems to go only to a business park.
You're on the bus tonight, headphones, synthetic waves,
Daryl Hall sings we've reached the borderline
By a terrace of little cottages made over *bijou*.
A large selection of other vehicles always available
Leaving Taunton on the M5. "Love will last forever."
In a thousand cities our offices are getting ready
To see that every transaction goes smoothly.
When the alarm sounds we go to assembly point D.
Agoraphobia, chronic anxiety, social phobia,
The narrator is bound up in some unspecified crisis.
When did the blue skies start to gather clouds?
How long have we poor shepherds lived and dreamed
Within these shady incremental pay-scales?

Blue Shift

You can tell by the landscaping we're off the route.
Two Sundays a month except for film shoots
And special picnics. Trees on a near vertical slope
As Caspar David leans on his staff and looks down.
The constant racket of cowbells clanging below,
Parachutes turning and floating across his view.
Pelargoniums on a wooden balcony
Over concrete. All this tends to repudiate
Positivist notions of historical fact
Now that the railways are run by enthusiasts.
To renew the experience of total fear
Only the genuinely random will do.
The doctor had Mussolini's brain in a jar
And we have an artichoke bubbling on the stove.

Well neither can I. We made our small gardens
Into an art wound up in video spools.
What if the index-linked audience stayed away?
What if the Sunday dune-painters were broke?
Some of them may want to be between channels
Full of garbled slogans and politics.
But the words did not glow, rather they were like braille
Punched into paper tape: finger tip experience.
Feel good in Lycra during work or leisure time.
I have trouble in mind: a prostituted and
Indiscriminate Romanticism. We choose
Weather-boarding because it smashes up so well
Be it in New England or on the Essex coast.
Go now: Let them try out this piece of action.

Frantic scenes were witnessed in Utopia
And important news was left out or "twisted."
Gazing over the visionary landscape, Joan sees
A brighter cloud from which emerges freedom:
The happy cry is taken up by the crowd –
With slimy shapes and miscreated life. It seems
A racist policeman planted the bloody rag
Giving the precise emotional push off. My eye
Turned westward, shaping in the steady clouds
Thy yellow sands and high white cliffs, O England
Ere from thy zephyr-haunted brink I turn . . .
On the cover was a blonde with a revolver
Falling from a window. When I asked him
The boy replied: "You just can't believe it."

But only the audience sees through the finish
Of surreal definition and heightened colour:
Gas explosion: black smoke: burning oil,
Scenes that we know but have almost forgotten.
It's a rapidly rotating column of air
Used to sell Swedish cars. A "control freak"
Would know all about airbags and crumple zones
In rapid and seamless transition. New actor
From La Jolla or anywhere else. Thunder storms.
A heavy steel box to cushion impact,
Swerve if you can, crates coming at you
On the runway. Thin faced but stylish in
Refugee chic, stubble cheekbones, accent.
Might just be a dummy on the test rig.

A nuclear reprocessing company
Makes a virtual shepherd working dogs
On a Lakeland hillside. Old head and staff
[Track in and zoom.] Over his shoulder we look down
Where a dog runs on lower ground. Green slopes
Fade to the everlasting universe of things
And the flat plane of the water. The blankness
Makes Patrick Caulfield look prophetic
Because the very blue resists absorption
As in the Luton airport flight simulator.
A passage to the limit in lurid carmine,
Then we go with divers and wavy deep stuff
The issues are remote handling and core values
Right out of Wordsworth's *Guide to the Lakes*.

How might you show his anxiety and suspense
By using different shots put together?
The golden cup appeared before me in the air
Sometimes the wrong way up, brimming high-key colour.
Ranging within the zodiac of his own wit
In that numbrous kind of writing called verse,
The human motif is almost entirely submerged
In the language of a Unitarian. Roses and moonlight.
The noise of a small group of carpenters
Building a staircase in another part of the studio,
We must find out what their motives are
Who call reason our guarantee of civil rights.
The definition of Somerset is the present boundary
Though Avon and Dorset will be opened up in '97.

A beginning wind strikes the aerial
And seeks striate closure in a foxy grid
As olives do colour the spirit body.
There were two of them floating over the water
And at times they would hold onto each other
You could barely see the movement of the wings.
Great daubs of paint from Kirchner to Kiefer.
Make a list of items mentioned in B not A.
She never told her love but let concealment
Like a worm in the bud feed on her damask cheek
Since too fast an inflation will break the neck
And too slow is dead as usual. Now
For which of the following reasons
Was the choice of husband or wife made?

The day is long without a schedule. Tell me
All the details that I didn't wish to know
It seems likely we'll find a treatment at last
Though he already scents thy footsteps in the snow.
This is the "clapper boy" as he is called
A dreamer not a rogue. It is the threat
Of being overwhelmed in too much writing
By which the energies of personal ambition
Are fed into the institutional machine.
Thwarted, baffled, and rescued in their own despite
Without powder or pomatum, whalebone or patches.
In unstressed syllables, however, it is not usual
For the y-element to be lost. The *yoo* sound
Is the only possible in *curlew* and *prelude*.

I clambered over boulders into a hidden combe
So dark and narrow under walls of steep rock
Much colder within where permanent snow
Slopes to the ridge above. There may be
Trouble ahead. Here are audit trails in the sky.
Gilpin would have owned it a horrid prospect,
Solitude itself. From the ridge Mont Blanc whelms up
Through piled cloud and beyond compare
Into hermeneutical sublime – whence ethics
Comes to the rescue of cognitive distress
And power in likeness of a helicopter
Comes down, scattering chamois in the ski slopes.
All of these emotions must be strange to you
Who shed tears of joy for life in the motley Strand.

What more would you have of me, say? Free drivers' kit?
Car sticker, tax-disc holder, map of properties
And windmills. Make life a breeze with direct debit.
(a) good looks, (b) wealth, (c) common sense,
(d) heroism, (e) good nature, (f) honesty,
(g) wife likely to be a good housekeeper,
(h) husband likely to be a steady fellow,
(i) success in sport or on stage or screen,
It's TV Stan, it's not supposed to be real.
The word "invisible" flames forth upon his chest.
Nice looking girl sniffs the dog food. Head of prisons
Sacked to protect the Home Secretary. So many
Novels turned inside out: "fly," "slug," "ant," "caterpillar,"
These trousers will maintain their shape throughout the day.

Non-Core Assets

They took a shadow and laid it in the straw.
Let it be rough and ready to make a reality
Deft, restless and unpredictable. Thus they rode
Through Norwich in every sort of fantastic dress.
Reason explained that good living was now over,
Time itself at hand. Lights, lanterns and fires
Burning in the woods. Damp air, shell-suit trousers,
Light blue sweatshirt, green padded jacket: the subject
Of this attack unknown. If you have no wire,
Roll newspapers into spirals, tie the ends together
In white cloth and herring skins. Thence souls in torment
Who do enter into these family customs
In schools, clubs or any organisation.
Among the straw cut-out is something of the truth.

They are like straight unwinding roads that lead
Into eternity. When we launch a car
We like to drop it. Root nourishing shampoo:
Dolphins ascending a water staircase.
Big coat and grip, gondola wedding,
Big coat and away through Lombardy poplars.
I find we have plenty of opportunities
For listening to speech, yet few people take them:
We need practical ways of securing resonance.
Urizen is at home on the world wide web
Sending pulses of self-indulgent grief echo
To measure your file space without hiring new staff.
A stretched limo floats over a crimson sunset
I never knew he missed driving so much.

Most districts have one or two damaged sounds
No longer so clear or pleasant as once they were.
Tunnels and sprinkler systems still provide good resin.
With its brown paper rocks, tinsel and silver,
This is renaissance style at its purest. Nice way
To put cash to work. *Sequoia gigantea* trees
Are older than Christianity and still alive,
But our best garden view is from the belvedere.
She or he was an evangelical angel
Preaching organisational entropy,
One step beyond employee empowerment –
And into virtual corporations. We find
A nostalgia for the social world of work
Unexploited as yet in direct sales.

Everyone who met those chosen lifters
Was seized by the arms, so that all strangers
Were forced to sign immunity certificates;
Crude, pitiful, and absurd as they were,
In clip-on ties to avoid being strangled.
When studying a sound, get to know all about it,
Use your eyes as well as your ears. A small
Pocket mirror will help you. The first time
That the voice of a dead witness was played in court:
"Just wanted to get the smirk off her face," he said.
It was our second steroid-abuse suicide.
Taking care will save your correspondent trouble.
A lively tongue makes for first class consonants,
It's useful to be a good telephone speaker.

Shoplifters encourage security staff
Who depend upon their continued activity. Strangers
Who may well have perfect immune systems,
Keep coming back for a pitiful loyalty bonus
And most victims were strangled in the park.
If you want steady growth you need sound money
Coming out of your ears. Like Leonard Nimoy,
She was always looking in the mirror,
According to our witness who travelled
Beside her in the train. Smile or smirk
It's hard to tell from this second-hand transcript
That maybe wasn't worth the trouble. I hoped
She would get over the tongue infection
And disinfect her telephone mouthpiece.

In this version the tale ends happily
Financed from operating cash flow over
The life of the contract. Destocking increases
Because of his wife's greed. He tricks and eats
A heron left to die out on the trading floor,
Moves into facilities management personnel,
Calculating to prevent costly down time
In non-core assets. His new stepmother
And her subsequent life with the dwarfs,
Cautiously rubbing salt into wounds,
And maintaining the final dividend in full
Before she walked out altogether. Start-ups
Have to be set against pump-priming write-offs,
Assuming the standard rate of income tax.

Better off separated, captured by tiny men
Who are at first hostile. They sell engines cheap
And make profits on spare parts. The brave tailor
Rescued by a hunter who asks hard questions
About indirect sex discrimination,
With a fine new frock, hairdo and glass slippers.
There is half a pound of salt in each body.
Enticed and outwitted by the witch
(Who likes a magic drink) Inky and the miser
Pushed her into an oven and discovered her
Sticky boards. The slow compromise of clarity
In workplace aesthetics. Second-half results,
When printed on double-perforated stock,
Can be run on a silent projector.

Later frames are photographs of places he knew
As they are today. His adventures with a whale
Before Snow White's birth: a flexible labour market
Where castles in the air take shape. New light
On the early life of Abraham Lincoln
Before his father remarried. Cordless,
Paperless, here and now: salary is salt
With text on the intervening frames.
Setting off on his good horse Rozinante
He faced quarrels with councillors over rats,
Money, and the enticement of children.
Budget box, wooden flute or feel-good factor
Takes us through the motivation peak cycle,
Who aspire to marry expanding markets.

A little Swiss girl at home in the mountains
Killed a two-headed giant and arranged
The staining and separate disposal of brains,
Skulls, thymus, spinal chord, tonsils, spleen,
And intestines. She beats the witch's curse,
Journeys far, escapes arrest by Despair,
Then unveils an underwriting profit
Photographed in natural scenery. Black Rod
Sees upbeat prospects in vacuum technology
For pure gases. His semiconductor plant,
Growing larger and smaller by magic,
Blows a chimney and spills waste in the river –
Taking objections lodged up to six months later.
Then he re-opens on a greenfield site.

The adventures by which I became rich,
Downsizing in local offices and HQ,
When all around had flipped. The genie in the cave
Showed me how to hold down subsidence payoffs.
Still hunting bears they were changed into stars,
Proving that job insecurity is a state of mind
Unrelated to the trauma of steel-closures.
Mortimer makes good, eaten by a sly old fox
And his twinkle-eyed boss. He wanted to marry
A pretty dancing girl or a bad tempered
Miserly elf. Sober bankers on the bridge
Of our struggling industrial flagship:
Remember the *Herald of Free Enterprise*
Turned on its side, duty-free shops and all, sinking.

Brought Forward

This is not the time to write as if you believe
In a time of writing. Most authors view cell death
As a landmark or end point for experiments
With other goals in distantly related fields.
So I would have it, letting the grass grow over
As we wade ashore in a costume re-enactment
Of the grand colonial adventure. We call it
"First landfall in Provincetown," after the event
Unsettled by a cautious trading statement.
Posing as messengers of an unknown nature
With all our cameras running: a repeat, a sequel,
Filming some years after *Apocalypse Now*.
The comparison between Prozac and Ecstasy
May well be misleading and irresponsible.

Most molecular data points towards
A lack of interest among teenage voters
In Ms Windsor and her relatives. Hindsight
Is a wonderful thing, the diet industry
A capitalist dream. They cut open the woman
And took out her living foetus. The killer said
That she wanted a baby of her own
Designed for the next millennium: nice chrome!
Two-year contracts become one-year rolling
Contracts when they expire. They follow
A programme towards their own death, reversible
By specific experimental manoeuvres.
Necrosis often affects whole sheets of cells
Their ghostly outlines remain long after the event.

Paparazzi on shopping trolleys peer over
Brick walls hoping to get one good shot
Before she departs for Argentina. They are
Unaware of immune surveillance systems.
It's day 107 of the Maxwell trial –
Rivals compare the free asset ratio
And pile into the stock. In long-term culture
Or immunological killing
Many forms of death may well exist
Causing immediate semantic problems
In key metabolic pathways. How like you this?
Power flotation will overshadow futures
Taking down the taper for family credit
As a consequence of uncontrolled survival.

Who pays taxes? Cords of viable tumour cells
And strangled profits for the main operators
Interspersed with zones of neurosis
Growing nicely thank you under the Beta field.
"This may involve some unforeseen social costs"
He said, in a kindly voice, keeping busy
With secateurs in the arboretum,
"Some lose water and condense, others swell and lyse."
98 acres to house 5700
Procurement officials, a new railway station,
MOD budget up. They all have to eat lunch.
Think of the local building spend, orbital roads,
DIY sales: let's dry-line and re-concrete
The cellar. Let's put down a patio.

In olden days we could have had her beheaded
And cultured *seriatim* indefinitely
For the top-end of the catering trade:
Watch out Aberdeen Angus, wild salmon,
Investors wanting capital guarantee.
Managers of personal equity plans
Ended the week with a bounce. Gold collar workers
Appear to be sensitive to stagging
And demand for securities is bound to rise.
Every decile in the poorest 50%
Does somewhat better, though we have no idea
How such a mechanism is evoked or what
Metaphoric signals trigger the call
By neighbouring cells for programmed suicide.

Acrimonious Funk, the alleged author of this
Catastrophe, was watching a very sad
Documentary about the fate of *Britannia*.
By that time we must have been at the party
Picking up regional specialities
From marquees sited at the enclave's edge
Which is when I began to smell freedom.
Women in head scarves pushing wheelbarrows
But all the men and teenage boys switched
To a January clear-out. Sub-couture touches
In the ethnic collection, a mix of synthetics
With a grubby *Virgin Atlantic* sweatshirt
Right out of the gym. For the cover we chose
A rusty railway track leading into a wood.

You may define a people by what they believe
And how they dance. For half in love with easeful death
They come to look at our experiments
To salvage from this debris. We walk the fields
Away from pretty homes and camp fires over
To the lonely place of our enactment.
Call it "remembering industry," call it
Anything you like. I seemed wise before the event
Because I had sole access to the statement.
These ceremonies are obsolete, like nature,
Like individual expression. The sequel
To life in our century begins about now.
Prospects are good for traders in ecstasy
Though predictions, I've heard, are irresponsible.

Not a family shot in the Christmas message
No queen of hearts. Burnt bodies in the woods
Laid out in star formation: peripheral
Target stimuli. A disused church, swords and flags,
Designed to be seen from the air. Workers for peace
Who cease upon the midnight with no pain
Finally robbed the morphine. Our heroine
Appears in a royal advert teaching orphans
To pronounce the queen's English: Spongiform
Encephalopathy Advisory Committee.
Sir Francis Drake sacked the city before this date
And is jolly in purple tights. We translate from
The original Greek into animation:
Not a family shot in the Christmas message.

Tuesday morning we worked out the press release
And consultancy agreement, privy to all
In the common room. A song that endures
On the dance floor with the deputy Master
And editor of criminal evidence.
Not a time to throw hats in the air. Mouth freezing
Small talk of our era. No news from the star chamber
But healthcare buildings coming onto the market
Should have a local effect. Last year's *Armani*
Turns over to a woman hanged in a wood
At Tuzla. Next move is to blast open an aid route
For those lorries full of sheep at Brightlingsea.
Hypo-allergenic stabilised retinol
Puts spice in the ex-bobbysoxers' ginger cake.

Shabby on tarmac, his one-time flatmate said to me
He was able to keep his off-road car because
All kinds of fluffy girlie things got in the way
Like threads unravelling in Petticoat Lane.
Freud knew "totem" as an Algonquian word
He turned into ready money. Nicotine patches:
He was good at getting ideas across, up to speed
On Muroroa. Think of Justus Liebig
Who in 1910 invented fluid beef cubes
When Virginia spoke of high expectations
In public life. A headless bronze "King and Queen"
Prepared in brine vinegar and olive oil
Wrapped in squares of aluminium foil
Making sure all trademarks are acknowledged.

Imitation of Life

If you are zinc deficient what you lose first
Is your sense of smell. Three human cases
Were chaotic rather than truly random
Due to tree-felling on the line. Ride into space
To wait an uncertain time in units called
Wave numbers. Disease erodes this memory.
I have seen Romanian shepherds piping
On TV, donnish yet funky prophets
Of deformed unshielded crystal. Too late
To convert speech into data packets,
Missing you already. Welcome to Heathrow's
Gate 31 automatic shopping mall.
Poles fall over and rot, why not leave them?
Chocolate and crisps to eat now or during your flight.

Two packs of melatonin, 15% off:
Because I'm worth it. The perfect start to a day.
He has allowed the substance known as poetry
To be infected with agents that inhibit
Pain receptors. The tongue touches an electrode
But we cannot yet in a ruinous place
Be confident. Here comes the science bit.
Narrower towards the front teeth, a main verb.
The same intrinsic brightness cannot be sustained
After the closing date. Happy perpetual flow
Of trivial objects, melted and reduced.
Long term unpredictability is a good sign.
Now they begin to sense their physicality
Most owners want their satellites out of this region.

This application form should be accompanied
By voice-mail and personal calls. Fair Athena,
It's easier if we don't see one another
And fold back separate pages. Each syllable
Proved difficult to unravel. These exist
For first and second persons only, and agree
Like adjectives. A moment white then melts forever:
It's your natural charisma that should shine through
Not your face. We did not pull down the city
Nor the city walls, for the goddess saved us.
Forget lip gloss, discover our new creation
Without expensive research. I had in my hand
A small engraving of orbital space junk,
Caviar blinis, a cigar owned by Churchill.

Trade in seahorses makes speech melt away
Like metallic paint, face down in the snow.
Volunteer stewards are needed. Beat to beat
fluctuations from healthy hearts. Permanent black
In the path of electron tunnelling. Who knows?
Low maintenance, the ultimate beauty
Principle. A dead region of tissue
Sits on six hydraulic legs in all-day colour
More radiant with every use. You need tangibles.
You need new sources of sustained revenue
Even if you're red-shy. When a white dwarf
Swallows gas, time increases from left to right:
Patch it into any existing submarine cable
With a live video feed. A slow business.

City vending invites you to refresh yourself
With a fresh-brewed 3D simulator package
That clamps over the shoulder. By knowing size
And age at maturity, you can do hand-held:
You can split chaos from pure noise or fold it back in.
Target species caught at sea by hand or in nets,
Lost to medicine forever. A new shipment
Requires its own newsletter to be set up
In woven nomadic colours. No longer feeds.
Soon we could all be eating it. Knowledge hunger
A sudden decline in muscle cells. Wet data
Always begins with some injury or need.
Narrative formats in our wet brains,
Extraterrestrial garbage. No longer breeds.

I looked up and saw big jet trails crossed in the sky
Evening light, smoke blowing across the stadium :
They told me, Heracleitus, you were dead.
I heard the attenuation of sound
Moving through the sample. This can also be
Retrofitted. They brought me bitter news to hear
And bitter tears to shed. The origin
Of this complexity has long been forgotten.
The article is not used with the predicate
And there is a new national mainline map.
This latest edition details more services.
The English words are not exactly as given
In the vocabulary. Think of synonyms.
They are chasing sailors into the market-place.

To the human eye, which cannot detect UV
That mental country is expected to decline
When compared with our thematic growth package.
War was unknown. Consumer groups approved
The packaged products and services of
Arethusa, who is the source of this sample.
Store in an upright position. London ivy
The natural and delicious alternative
Sits awkwardly on screen. Asian tigers
Fail to bounce back for the demise of inflation.
Trainer and jockey in the best of form
Who wander into the Arcadian sunlight
Found in direct speech. One trillion bits per second.

Nothing works like repression in fixed circuits
To carry signals to the heart. Enjoys music,
Gardening, cinema, seeks funny male
Who must be genuine. Unlimited access,
Staggered vesting facilities, spin resonance
Left on the verge. The next crash in Tom-all-Alone's
May perpetuate the notion of brevity
But not always in pentameter. A final
Brief chapter. No mention of another fix.
We're launching plain vanilla funds no longer
Relax and feel the benefit. Well strung-out,
A stream which flowed underground for many years
Revealing the personality. No pine trees
Were felled to make keels. No walls surrounded cities.

It's the most selfish act. Struck by a laser beam
The second and fourth lines of each stanza
Opt for income drawdown. A verbatim replay
Emerged in Syracuse but fails to reach
The rest of the body. Don't underestimate
Your gut feeling. More radiant with every use,
The backward glance, the fragile equilibrium.
Are you sleep deficient? We seek no discount
But actual acquaintances of the poet
In waves of electrical excitation.
Knowledge of transgenic breeding is useful
As non-humans are not able to do this
For themselves. He draws on his aerospace background
For the reality of mud and trailer camps.

If the wave breaks apart, strict repetition
Saves exhausted and contaminated paper
On the Etruscan ridges. They never knew
What they were working on. It was simple
Competing for space on oestrogen receptors:
Silicon is the normal base. We'll call her
Princess DNA. The actual words
Reappear in the previous paragraph.
Hundreds of captives transported to Persia.
A man around whom complications gather
At the end of a long bull market. Camilla
Was a Volscian nursed by a wild mare
And with her shaft of pine she ran him through.
Tiny rings of DNA are killing us all.

Restricted Zone (slight return)

How could the mind take hold of such a country
In which white heaps build up and ivy covers
The early industrial era? Chimneys seem
To contain many things long and short. No smoke
From these abandoned engines. Wires converge
On a ring attached to a wooden pole
With ceramic fittings. "Someone's with me in RL,"
It said, "Ask Janine about her new ID."
Plastic moulded into bone-shaped buttons.
A small noun, head down in a damp field,
Cropping verbs uncovered in the present
Continuous. Beyond the bullet-proof glass
He smiles and waves – our man in developing states –
Coming down on liberation theology.

Luminous rape under grey cloud shows red
In the satellite heat picture. We're proud of our people.
A yellow shirt on platform five explodes the subject,
Testing visual and orthographic processing.
Policies based on instruments such as green-belt
Have little effect on the shape of metropolis.
Every neighbourhood in parameter space
Finds the nearest periodic attractor. Innovation,
Technical know-how, attention to detail –
Casting the French-polisher from *Yellow Pages*
For his trusty face. A sleep-out on Mt Igman
With a minimum four hundred knots to the inch.
Snow holes, barbecue, good definition
In fractal clusters grown using local rules.

5AM on the tree-lined campus
As scholars arrive in the back seats of taxis
Met from the sleeper train, still a bit sleepy,
Radiators, shelves, glass – things just falling.
We ran to the toilets for cover, hoping
For a little shut-eye ahead of registration
If the porter would open up a study-bedroom.
Just an accident of where you live and how
You hold a pencil, listening for metal wheels
Hitting joints in the rails, car horns each to each.
Streets are familiar but not quite right,
A fine blue morning with high cloud.
The rabbits up early, out on the lawns
Ready to feed and have their photos taken.

This is the beginning of a poetry conference.
Linen trousers are supposed to look as if
You slept in them. Windows sucked out of buildings
A quarter of a mile away. We took it
Back to focus group 21, weighed down
With items for the delegates' book table;
Whether relaxing, doing odd jobs round the house,
Or out and about in the car. Still sleepy
On *Glenfiddich* and *Temazepam*.
Getting rid of a pocket full of pound coins
Is a good idea, in the centre of Manchester
Or any city. Your open container
Drips onto plastic mulch. Red flow from a car boot:
All you do is listen and the stories come to life.

In multitudinous chatterings, she sees through
Simulation to the bone – pity and fear
Is what we feel, working through outmoded systems:
What else can a mother give her daughter?
A beautiful riff in time, say March in 44 BC.
Lost incomprehensible affect, lost feelings,
Truth lies hidden in a deep unfashionable well.
Years when Italy was torn. Therefore I resign
All claim to this experience, reading,
Writing, sailing a boat, getting hit on the head
In not-quite unison. Uffington white horse
Cut in the iron age. Photo by *Aerofilms*.
But since ferns have no seed, where would you cast them,
Knowing that each single angel is terrible?

The coiled wires are red, yellow and green
Running from the cab. Let's set up a phone-in.
Biting through leaves, tarpaulin, and good rope
To arrive at Brodmann's areas 44/45.
An infectious protein that attacks the brain
Known as a prion. Surviving heat treatment,
We are still hoping to make our connection
Following a white line and red lights ahead.
A complex pattern of frequency-locking
Is better than no pattern at all. *Air Ride Suspension.*
Systems with many degrees of freedom
Such as turbulent fluids, fibrillating hearts,
Movements of populations in real cities:
This medium makes gender surfing possible.

This is how we stabilise a chaotic array
In neurologically normal right-handed males:
From permutation to negativity
A simple but non-trivial pattern emerges
Which cannot be called unconscious.
Breathing in small particles of you, which
Already have their receptors, so that
When you raise an arm to push back your hair
And shift slightly in your seat, aware or not,
The faintest trace upon the air invents
This utterance. She would pronounce "semiotic"
Licking the moisture off and causing more
To arrive. The number of pixels showing
Activation in the inferior frontal gyrus.

I recollect the council was going green
And we announced it right after the phone-in
On the Auschwitz bus-trip. Give them more rope
And play-back time. Being born before '45
Was a basic qualification. No brain-
Dead Surrealists, no special treatment:
Neo-modernists break their own connections
Or drop off the classics list. We will stay ahead
Only by vocabulary-locking.
The future is bright, with temporal suspension,
Wir machen den weg frei: customer freedom
Is the feeling we hope for in all our hearts.
Country weekends, trouble free return to city
Apartments: let us make your dream possible.

Thus troubled clergy in the northern diocese
Learnt the boundaries of clerical morality.
"Dual containment" looks increasingly futile
To a palsied youth locked into a war game
Scenario. His car crashed, clothes ablaze,
Who did not close his eyes for seven days
But continued to steer and use the foot-pedals,
Cutting out some heavy-handed melodrama,
Which floats in a pool of light on Dundee's stage.
Bombing speaks to no-one but pushes up prices
And frightens the children. We brought them back
With careful friendly speech, then hypnotherapy,
In a corner flat in building 132.

You can lock up kids but it doesn't change
Behaviour patterns. Here comes the Euro:
Plenty of soft edges, moving to Dagenham.
The ward was filled with amputee children
Meeting the deficit target. Worries about
The peaceful integration of disparate states
Are irrational. Genetic engineering
Helps to make sure the output gap is clawed back:
The safety of your corn plant is unfounded.
Now that self-assessment is approaching
You need to put some instruments in place: invest.
We don't shoot the messenger. Now find the umbrella:
A target for Serbian shells. This guarantee
Does not affect your statutory rights.

Speckled Noise

Give me intimate and penetrating studies
Of human behaviour, engineered leak-proof
In a thick but appropriate magenta.
It's hard to imagine an easier or more
Intuitive system. Their jewelled ear-rings
Screwed tight into unpierced ears, depend upon
The very language of the fish market
Which deters the meanest rash action. It was
No ordinary Monday bought in ready-made
Since we cut back on location dramas.
Well sourced or not, it's all interpretation:
Whether you play the standards to old tunes,
Or in a sudden frenzied modernity, seek to
Become the grunge idol of a million slackers.

We would promenade, when some curious passer-by
(In feathers raped from the osprey) was heard to say,
"How do birds smell red or hear green?" Let me tell you
It was no such uncommon thing to be blinded
By the extreme vividness of their exterior;
Some startling and quite pointless convolution of
Blue muslin, yellow hair and high quality drama.
No-one wants to be a teenager anymore.
These holographic images are heat-stable
But readily erased by circularly
Polarised light. Now conceive you a great passion
And loftiness of manner in this lamentably
Absurd lapse from verity. So: wheezing, sneezing,
Came in the small men with black and rosy faces.

I travelled with that worthy gentleman
Who brought over a patent under the broad seal
For our governance. Addicted to late dinner
He employed a sabbatical vocalist
To sing only anthems and oratorios
And inaugurate the winter season. So I
Experienced the higher than ambient flux
In equatorial pacific. I found me
Isotopic traces of export production:
Continental dust preserved in ice cores
Of Greenland and Antarctica. Such a muffled
And musty smell came from his adopted frock-coats
Beneath gothic canopies of fumed oak
In our artistic and half-timbered cafes.

You may wonder why our ready-gel is causing
So much excitement, since there is more news
Than a paper has room to print. Impossible
Assertions occlude the real purpose of the work
Which leaked out of the banking system. Normally
A liquidator is appointed but buyers
Get no compensation. Simply collect 8 tokens
And join the queue for post-war restitution
(Don't even ask about the price of dental work.)
Lawyers, notaries and fiduciaries have all
Just been lonely too long. Not a nail on the wall –
No chair, no table, no straw mattress, nothing.
But they did not concede that this was the amount
Held back with vast sums of production money.

These then were the lessons of American
Narrative process, script driven, whose unspoken
Allegation of transcendentalised high tea
Faded like an old sugared biscuit in a
Second-empire scheme of chocolate, turquoise-
Blue and gold. Benefits include personal calls
Office sex, internet access – it's a sad day
For investigative journalism. She/he sang
"I want to be a cowboy's sweetheart, for they
Are so expressive in their dress and adornments."
Our strongest impression was a kindly
Timidity: tinkle, trill and sweetly jingle,
Silly as any alpine cowbell you may hear
In one of those old-time menthol tobacco ads.

The review is broken into two parts
Each of which begins with an oversized drop-cap
To introduce this fairy tale of nothingness.
They put to sea with a prosperous wind, and now
Being compact together in one ship, declare
It is not enough to call for *northern sunlight*
We must demonstrate our serious commitment
To support, deliver and reward these ladies
Of fabulous age, celebrity scholars and
Post-modern architects. Language such as "soothe"
"Calm" and "reasoned" reinforces this tendency
More steadily as the election approaches.
A dramatic increase in phytoplankton growth
Turns the sea at last from blue to green.

And this fine emancipatory thought was come
On my afternoon walk, so that at once I saw
The advantage of raking, indeed enfilading,
The promenade with its south-facing windows.
Sister Midnight, who looked severely at the band
Sporting a corraline stethoscope, told us
Her house had become "a perfect museum." She was
Trading off-plan conversions of inner-city
Old industrial buildings, getting in the way
Of small random errors in voting intentions.
Total RNA blots, prepared with RNA
From human tumour, foetal and normal tissue,
Are pre-tested to ensure the presence of
Full-length transcripts. We will where possible avoid
The expense of pursuing judicial reviews.

A gentle push of cam closures fastens the gate
And guides cattle to the crusher for de-horning
Without undue pain. We have outstanding
Image brightness, motorised photo-functions,
Absolute data security. How about
This millennial project? A virtual building –
No gravity or planning disputes, open to all.
No-one has been murdered on London's underground
As yet. Editing numbers appear on each frame.
In the world of viruses, we are invaders.
This skylight speech is no accidental figure
taken up for eloquence and now abandoned
In some dumb remake of *Clueless*. You're stuck inside
The engine room of the knowledge society.

We crawled on bubble plastic in the roof space
(A new performance, this) so that try as we may
There was quite a racket in the engine room.
But we needed an experienced oracle
Developer, designer or analyst
To set up the cash cow, extended warranties,
Little beads drifting in magnetised fluid.
Gradually this uncertain chronology
Hardened into historical record, so that
We were stuck with sclerotic it. A group tour
In front of an 11 foot screen, steering
With a joystick. We could follow the adventures of
Mary Kingsley who, armed with an umbrella,
Foraged among mangrove swamps seeking specimens.

When through blue lips they murmured that a paper
May well switch allegiance, it was news to some
Apparently. Best chill the rice before you stir-fry
Drifting gradually eastwards. How was it
That such a fortunate concatenation
Of circumstances came to be? Why not eat speech?
A method of seismic energy transfer,
You mix it up with vegetables and red ink.
Go on: popular culture binds us together
If anything does. Gerunds like Gladstone bags
Remind us of long dead politicians who
Develop through controlled underground explosions
Or outmoded travel accessories. Meaning
Is something we lost back in 1973.

Always Read the Label

This body does not contain an index, but is
Otherwise spontaneous, unrestrained, natural –
Made from the finest time-dated TV footage :
Ironic, absurd, full of self mockery. Shot
In one of those rambling clapboard houses
Like a brilliant parody of criticism
Which says nothing at all. Shut the jewel case.
Belief in God may not be sufficient protection
For the under-capitalised, so that
The following year you'll be back where you started
In a blood-spattered cowshed. You can leave early
(Weather permitting) float into a delirium.
"Shut the jewel case like a good boy" she said,
"History just doesn't happen everywhere."

You begin not by picking up the powerbook
But by deciding to begin. Here we are
Established in a freezing pinch of the feet.
The smoke bush is another example.
Inuit are at the top of their food chain
In the ultimate chemical dump. Boil water,
Cook your meat right through, demand a second ballot.
You can't get a solution by proxy
In any aspect but the purely visual.
These are real flaws in the non-profit ethic
To which is subjoined the machinery of this
My eclogue, old and well publicised in the night sky.
The entire braid can be coded as a sequence
And thus receive your troubled delegation.

Patrick was the name of the day as I heard it –
Slide into the seat, put your hands at the wheel
And feel our glorious Teutonic past. No bugs.
A fabulously elliptical house style.
Governments control this data. There will be no
Opportunity for lunch. Small business users
Are welcome on the field trip to St Elizabeth's
With chill-out rooms for true skaters. Our psychodrama
In a strange labyrinthine palace of ice.
It means something like "deep home" but with overtones
Of hatred and loathing. Things and persons always
Already alien. The worst fears of researchers:
Forests haunted by shapeless apparitions
From the middle-England mail-order catalogue.

Why is it that a man seems so sinister
Wearing gloves indoors? Someone says "mind the gap"
As he moves along measuring table settings.
These are things and persons always already
Innocent in the soft verges. Don't leave the lights on –
They will kill you for a shovelful of small coals.
Martha, the world's last passenger pigeon, long dead.
Soft-feel fibres and drizzle-paint, pink on light brown.
This glass is wrapped for your personal use
It won't last so call Stewart. Gold in your teeth.
A floor-proximity guidance system
Will direct you to the exit. Remain seated.
Call Anne today on a quiet cul-de-sac.
Double car port, cheaper than renting, call Eddy.

Unsteady on his legs in Omega cottage,
He bent down to pick up the lion. This set,
A translated grove with low maintenance
Corals and sponges, comes with deep-yellow flicker.
She wiped the points of her nail-scissors to retard
Clonal reproduction and complete the crossword.
A Canadian cadence to that voice. Red or green?
Slipping on wet marble slabs, we look up
At the LCD information panel. No trains.
Asda price, pocket the *différance*. Replace
The mindset. Up the broad avenue into town
Obviate the need for costly simulations.
The explicit limit of our instructions is
That the icon convey mean time to extinction.

Call it a "family" toothbrush, spin on about
Delicate gum tissue (bleeding round the teeth)
In the later bracketed line. Let's go for
Rapid expansion out of Protestant theory:
Quality, Deep House and Trance. "More relaxed" still means
The perfect "more relaxed" outfit. You'll need gloves
And a tank for surgical waste. Ishi, the last
Wild Indian of California, spent his
Days in the anthropological museum –
He just couldn't cope with San Francisco.
You can phone researchers and tell them your story
In unannotated regions of *E. coli*
Chromosomes. Transcripts completely updated and
Tastefully landscaped. Buy now, choose your own colours.

From time to time we may pass on your name
To other, carefully selected companies
That ferry impulses above the brain stem.
No live model could stay in place night and day.
Please select another channel. Pull the mask
Towards you and breathe normally to download
A fully-functional demo version. At the epoch
Of last scattering, ordinary matter
Was dumped all over the Hubble sphere.
Now the dim gods of death have in their keeping
Mere protein fragments. You take out bone marrow
Add your viral vector, put the bone marrow back.
Palatino is fine – but I prefer Caslon.
It's a genuine pleasure having you on board.

Dummies sometimes take the place of real people
To see how badly they might have been hurt.
We encourage you to watch the video
Which is for your own welfare. Everything downstream
Of the blood clot was either politically
Unstable or subject to hormonal surges.
It was "extremely unlikely" that the canisters
Could have broken up in the atmosphere.
What if the Continuity Army Council
Neither consented nor refused to complete the trade?
If no Wimbledon train is shown, take the next
Dimmer switch that comes on gradually
In foetal development. Pressure of light
Produces gold-plated stars. When does pain begin?

The so-called nonsemantic features of language
Never had time to be beautiful. Hold fingers
Horizontally touching your forehead
To show the amount. Tongue and groove boarding
In a plausible context, one of the plots
Is newly dug. These are voluntary targets
A little nonplussed by your stoical charm
Having issued writs, free pens and mouse mats.
A strip of brain tissue that hugs the surface
Causing a massive increase in drag. Implants could
Translate prejudice directly into votes:
A whole panel of buttons that must be pushed.
Pain without cognition. No other network
Covers more of the UK population.

Britain, perfect for filming period drama
And convenient for *Eurodisney*, appears
To be rising more slowly. The prospect of ermine
Keeps eclipsed former ministers in order;
Reducing the appearance of wrinkles, which are
Broader and deeper than one might expect,
Marching into the second chamber. Hello John.
When the hounds of spring are on winter's traces
There may be no mortgage and no purchase
Despite low entry and exit costs. Most victims
Were homeless men sleeping rough but holding fast
To core principles. Sleet threatened, snow was alleged –
Broadcast on two cable networks. Making the dream
A reality, surrounded by spotty dogs.

Radial Symmetry

The reliquary of St Chad contained bones from
Three legs which, if not in actual ownership,
Comprised a new threat to passenger safety.
Guerrillas spent the early days of the siege
Watching TV for the first time. Here the weary
Traveller will find stress and memory loss
In abandoned and vandalised public parks.
List brokers selling shareholders' names. Such products
Appeared in most industrialised countries
And provided a notion of community
For branded global foods. 7000 vehicles
Under spotlights behind razor-wire fencing:
People firing bullets into the air. Soft drinks.
The confidential odour of enormous books.

Narrative must persist beyond such events
Or we should float unanchored and rudderless
In some unfathomable sea. Headless statues
Made over by an image consultant
From the consistory court. You'll find them both
In my Indian bag. About 70 genes
Have not been deleted so far: hundreds of men
Came out of the ground in foraging parties,
And hybrid fertility is very low.
I was enjoined to eat a good breakfast before
DNA-testing of the relics of saints
In a commercial plantation. A new, higher,
Homozygotic peak, like a wasp in a lyric
Whenever Hamilton's rule is satisfied.

It was a chill, blue-fingered hour and the gardens
Were nearly empty, as will often be true
In structured or viscous populations. After
Some agonising moments with hairpins, we
Attended to a paper on rapid changes
In the geological record. These "pages"
Were not pages at all but information dumps
Big as Bayreuth backdrops. Such variation
May be "factored out" to reveal a new reading
Of male relationships running through the book.
Stylish, slim M, played with immense authority
Seals his grip on the party. Pools of selected
Mutant genes produce a tremendous performance
Of baffled resentment: a cow for a few beans.

All these methods are seriously flawed.
Extinction probability is a product
Of fitness and speciation. Whether or not
Wrecked car parts stacked on rooftops constitutes
A planning violation, we should move away.
Disaster movies need terminal sequencing.
You may not reach adaptive optima
Or resist repeated invasion by clones.
The American civil war stopped the export
Of cotton. Are we a nation of shoplifters?
Stylish, fair, slim. Easygoing F, 36.
Male-biased dispersal, direct no-nonsense style.
"I want to live in the future," he says,
Painting eyes on a transparent screen.

This herring is a pretty fish. We are looking
At the degree of ornamentation beyond
Future survival prospects. An individual
Could be a sterile worker, isolated by
Distance and genetic redundancy, outwith
The rim of standard English. Post-segregational
Killing is not a unique function of surface
Exposure, but we have yet to run
A capital needs analysis. Little drops
Of lavender water, a minute handkerchief
Gritty with lace. Ancient conserved protein families.
Whatever leaks from the reference pile.
Many of these are careful and exquisite
Now that ashes serve to thicken his mixes.

The unofficial shortlist, taped to my windscreen,
Looked like a threat. Who cares what the magistrate says
For moral guidance? We advise selling old-style
Government offices. Open at thirty-six
Million. Come down heavy on shoplifters.
We could demerge tomorrow. The word "export"
Indicates higher alcohol level. These clones
Are fed to their lean bodyweight optima.
Bioremediation is about sequencing
Of nutrients: bacterial take-away
Hoovers up the oil spill. None of this constitutes
A written contract and the supplier will not
Be responsible for loss beyond product
Value. Why was our market intelligence flawed?

Who decided to air freight Egyptian beans?
How much can we lose? So-called high performance
Investment funds prey on carefully selected
Undervalued companies. No authority
Can protect border-crossing species. This new book
Will help you to overcome fear of reading
Aloud. Value criteria variations
As a method of corporate change. No-one dumps
In local rivers anymore. We have pages
Running next to features you'll love. Money changes
Hands. Discreetly filmed and interviewed, we
Loved to watch ourselves shopping. This was after
Double vouchers and cashback. Can it be true?
A year's free subscription to *Royal Gardens*?

Based at our vibrant and informal offices,
You would enjoy free permanent health insurance,
Money recycling, preferential share options.
Robin Hood has changed sides. Power lines above
Permanent way. Deep in the rain forest he finds
Polynesian families watching London news:
Cross-border Christmas shopping down 80 percent.
Evidence from tree-rings, pollen analysis,
and other paleoclimate records shows that
Normal healthy sperm production follows
The lunar cycle. Earth must have encountered
Dense clumps of dark matter in space. We have
Genome data from *Escherichia coli*
Served on a bed of seasonal leaf salad.

Some of these points, known as seismic gaps, are explained
As simple outcomes of random processes
Swallowing up identity. We ask them
To re-enact their purchases whilst we measure
Pupil dilation and subsequent aftershocks
In a region known as the outer rise. Butter
Trickles down his leg. Was Magwitch a paedophile?
Where are the wild export markets that used to be?
Most of these drugs are obsolete. Breakdown products
From a detergent used in the manufacture
Of paper, textiles and plastics. Oestrogens
Somehow leaking into the water supply.
With practice you'll wake up right inside the action
And experience the dream as real as your life.

A smooth laminar stream dissolved the surface.
Mist drifted over the pool of London. I woke
In the abstract sea of unspecified emotion.
Big tour operators are working to patch this
Through a headset. An uncle running up to bowl,
Someone sampling smut. Taste of lemons and oysters.
Music has downsized in tune with the casual look
Now transcending fashion as such. Radiation
And sudden exposure to market forces
Stripped out early consumer activity.
Should another mail arrive from Europe today
Be sure to be clear that we have completely
Conflicting visions of the future. Tick if you
Would prefer not to receive this material.

Index

Aberdeen Angus 55
abstract 29, 110
Aerofilms 75
aerospace 69
After Lorca 23
Air Ride Suspension 76
Albertine 26
Algonquian 60
Alleghenies 16
America i, 19, 29
Anne 94
Annie Apple 5
Antarctica 83
Apocalypse Now 51
Arcadia 1, 67
Arethusa 67
Argentina 53
Armani 59
Asda 95
Asian 67
Athena 63
Atlantic 14–15, 56
Auschwitz 78
Autumn 11, 23
Avon 36
Bayreuth 103
beans 103, 107
belvedere 43
Benson, Steve 25
Berrigan, Ted 16
Beuys, Joseph 17–18
Berwick-upon-Tweed 8
Beta field 54
Bioremediation 106
Black Rod 49
Bonnard, Pierre 23
Bourgeois 5–6
Braille 32
Brightlingsea 59
Britannia 56
Brodmann's areas 76
Browning, Robert 21
Burroughs, William 26

Caddel, Richard 113
Camilla 70
Cantos, The 18
Cape Cod 17
Care in the Community 27
Caslon 97
Caulfield, Patrick 35
Caviar blinis 63
chaos 65
Chimneys 71
Chinese 18
Chocolate 61, 85
Christianity 43
Christmas 58, 108
Churchill, Sir Winston 63
Clueless 88
cognitive distress 39
colours 65, 96
consumer 67, 110
Continuity Army Council 98
cotton 104
crumple zones 34
crusty 11
Dagenham 80
Danse du feu 26
dark matter 108
Day, Jean 25
Deep House 96
de Kooning, Willem 21
Destocking 46
Diana, Princess 16, 70
di Benedetto, Steve 113
différance 95
DNA 10, 70, 102
Dorset 36
Downsizing 50
Drake, Sir Francis 58
Dundee 79
Eagle 10
Ecstasy 51, 57
Egyptian 107
Elgar, Sir Edward 7
enclosures acts 2

[113]

England 14, 32–33, 93
Essex 32
eternity 42
Etruscan 70
Eucalyptus 18
Euro 80
Eurodisney 100
Eurotunnel 21
False Memory 15
fiduciaries 84
Fisher, Allen 114
French 5–6, 72
Freud, Sigmund 60
Friedrich, Caspar David 31
Friesian 12
frontal gyrus 77
Funk, Acrimonious 56
Gardening 68
geese 9
Georgics, The 29
Gilpin, William 39
Gladstone, William 90
Glenfiddich 74
global 101
God 91
Greek 5, 58
greenfield 49
Greenland 83
grunge 81
Guide to the Lakes 35
hairpins 103
Hall, Daryl 30
Hamilton's rule 102
Handel 26
Harryman, Carla 114
Harvard 17
Heathrow 61
Helvetica 18
Heracleitus 66
Herald of Free Enterprise 50
herring 41, 105
historical record 89
History 91
Home Secretary 40
Horace (Quintus Horatius Flaccus) 27
Hubble 97

Implants 99
indus opaque 22
Irish box 13
Ishi 96
Italy 19, 75
Janine 71
Jeffers, Robinson 16
Keats, John 57–58
Kerridge, Richard 114
Kiefer, Anselm 37
King and Queen 60
Kingsley, Mary 89
Kirchner, Ernst Ludwig 37
La Jolla 34
Lakeland 35
lemons 110
liberation theology 71
Liebig, Justus 60
Lincoln, Abraham 48
lip gloss 63
liquidator 84
Lombardy 42
London ii,4,67,88,108,110
Luton 35
Lycra 32
MacSweeney, Barry 114
magenta 81
Magwitch 109
Main Street 22
major 5
Major, John 8
Management 3, 46
Martha 94
Maxwell, Robert 53
Meaning 13, 90
Mengham, Rod 114
menthol 85
metabolic pathways 53
metropolis 72
Minerva 10, 22
Moby Dick 16
MOD 54
Mont Blanc 39
moonlight 36
morphine 58
Mortimer 50
Mt Igman 72

[114]

Muroroa 60
Mussolini, Benito 31
Narrative process 85
Necrosis 52
Neo-modernists 78
New Abjectionists 24
New dawn 26
New England 32
Nimoy, Leonard 45
Norwich 41
nothingness 86
Oliver, Douglas 115
Omega 95
Oscar Orange 5
osprey 82
oysters 29, 110
Pain receptors 62
Palatino 97
parody 91
Patrick 35, 93
pay-scales 30
Pelargoniums 31
Persia 70
Petticoat Lane 60
phytoplankton 86
Pittsburgh Memoranda 16
poetry 14, 28, 62, 74
Pound, Ezra 18, 47, 74
Princess DNA 70
promenade 82, 87
prospect 10, 39, 100
protein families 105
Provincetown 51
Prozac 51
purple tights 58
Queen of hearts 58
rabbits 73
Radicals 5-6
Radio tracking 9
random 31, 61, 87, 109
ready-gel 84
Reagan, Ronald and Nancy 16
reality 41, 69-100
Redman, Dewey 115
Redwood, John 21
retinol 59
Riley, Peter 115

RL 71
Robin Hood 108
Romanian 61
Romanticism 32
Rosa Mundi 26
Royal Gardens 107
Rozinante 48
Saatchi, Maurice 14
San Francisco 96
second ballot 92
Serbian 80
sex discrimination 47
shoplifters 45, 104, 106
Siena, James 115
Sierra 7
simulator 35, 65
Sister Midnight 87
slug-horn 21
Small business 93
Somerset 3, 36
Spaghetti vongole 23
St Chad 101
St Elizabeth's 18, 93
stagging 55
Stan 40
star chamber 59
Star-gazy pie 13
steroid-abuse 44
Stewart 94
Strand 39
study-bedroom 73
subsidence 50
Surrealists 78
Swedish 34
Syracuse 69
tarmac 60
Taunton 30
teenager 82
Temazepam 74
Thatcher, Margaret 15
Thoreau, Henry 16
Tom-all-Alone 68
Totnes 1
Trance 19, 96
trousers 40-41, 74
Tuzla 59
Uffington 75

[115]

Ugolino, Lorenzetti 28
umbrella 80, 89
Unitarian 36
Urizen 42
Utopia 33
UV 67
Value criteria 107
Virgin Atlantic 56
Virginia 60
viruses 88
Volscian 70
Wagner, Richard 19
Warner, Rex 14
Water bombs 1
Watten, Barrett 116
whalebone 38
white dwarf 64
White, Snow 48
Williams, Serena 116
Wimbledon 98
Windsor, Ms 52
Wordsworth, William 35
workplace 47
wrinkles 100
Yale 17
Yellow Pages 72
Young, Geoffrey 116
Yo-yo Man 5
Zeus 4
zodiac 36

Printed in the United Kingdom
by Lightning Source UK Ltd.
9577100001B